I JUST WANT TO MAKE YOU LAUGH

ANNA NAAX

I JUST WANT TO MAKE YOU LAUGH

Copyright © 2014 ANNA NAAX

Editing by Angela Smith

Book Design by Danor Shtruzman

All rights reserved. This book or any portion thereof may not be reproduced or used in any manner whatsoever without the express written permission of the publisher except for the use of brief quotations in a book review or scholarly journal.

Some of the names have been changed to protect their identities. Yes, the author's dog's lawyer suggested to changed their names so they won't be known.

Please note this is the author's first time writing. She barely passed her English classes. The author is also having a hard time writing this paragraph in third person. Also, take into consideration the editor of this book is not a professional. She just really loves to read and thought it would be a fun project to help out her friend.

The editors described in this book are an illusion. When Editor 1 is describe, that is Angela Smith, and when Editor 2 is mentioned that is in fact the author of this book, the marvelous Anna Naax.

ISBN-10: 150064840X
ISBN-13: 978-1500648404

To everyone who made an impact in my life

Thank you for all the inspiration and support you have given me

ACKNOWLEDGMENTS

I would also like to thank wine. I love you wine. If I could marry you I would. You are so delicious but I can only handle you in small quantities so maybe we shouldn't get married. I don't think anyone reads this part of the book. That's okay though. This section is for you wine even though the wedding is off.

PREFACE

I am receiving many guidelines on how to write this preface section. Let's go over them together! The first one says that the author writes the preface. Okay, I got the first check mark done! I, the writer, am writing the preface. This is a great start for me!

The second step is to write about some information that is essential to understanding the book and is also a spot for the author to speak directly to the reader. Hello reader, I am speaking to you! If you can't tell I'm waving at you right now. This is a great time to visualize me waving frantically at you through the words you are reading. As far as telling you critical information about my book, all I can say, it's funny as hell. I hope that is "essential understanding" enough. All I want to do is make you laugh. You might roll your eyes or even shake your head at some of it but make sure you smile and laugh.

My inspiration for writing this book was out of boredom. Literally, I was bored and I started to write a book. Technically it wasn't this book but I couldn't finish a paragraph of a fiction novel. A good friend of mine said I could write a memoir type of book. And here it is in your hands. Well, it might be in your tablet but it is still in your hands. Now that I think about it, my book could be on a tablet that's not in your hands. Okay, your eyes are on it. There, much better.

Anyway, I have many inspirations why I have decided to publish this book. Among those are close friends and people I have never met. I loved writing this book and I hope you enjoy reading it! Go my friends! Read my book and

laugh because that's all I want you to do!
.

THE FIRST CHAPTER

Welcome to the first chapter! I could have also named it the introduction. My lack of ability falls on this part where I'm supposed to tell you all about myself. Lets see... right now I'm on my second bottle of wine trying to think how to write a book that might never get published all while I'm staring aimlessly at that third bottle of wine calling my name from the kitchen. Perhaps one more glass and the words will start flowing. One moment. There that's much better. Wine is so delicious. I am pondering the question of "*why the hell would I buy three bottles of wine at once?"*

    I am a student which means I am poor and it also means I have a drinking problem. The problem being I can't afford it (unless it's really cheap). A major reason I'm writing this book is because I would love to be a comedian as a side job rather than working with the general public who are normally in a bad mood and wear way too much perfume. I love to make people smile and laugh about stupid things and stupidity it self. I just might finish that last bottle of three-dollar wine now just for the hell of it!

INAPPROPRIATE BEHAVIOR

Ever see men adjusting their privates? I have and I can tell you I am always appalled when I see them do that. It puts a bad taste in my mouth for unknown reasons that you might be assuming right now. Gross. Get your mind out of the gutter! It's just so…inappropriate.

If you haven't noticed, women adjust too! I do it all the time, and I don't care who is watching (well I do a little). No, I don't mean adjusting my balls; I don't have those. I have boobs and from what my friends say, they are pretty big. They also say they are very jealous because they want my size of tits. I would gladly donate mine any day!

One day when I was chasing my dog, who was chasing a squirrel, I had to stop and adjust the titties (they were trying to get out of their nest). It's very uncomfortable when they fall out of the bra like that. It's especially uncomfortable when one boob is half in and half out of the bra too.

Usually when a woman has to adjust they do it discreetly, and only when no one is looking (or so they think). If one tit gets way out of line you can try to knock it back into place with a slight graze of the arm. Usually that doesn't work. So the next attempt is you can pull the bra up and out through the shirt with a quick snap of the wrist and hopefully those escape artists will fall back where they need to be. But lets face it, women have to mold them to the right position. Since when do tits "fall" where they should be? There's always a molding process. (Now that I think of it, if I were to get a boob job I bet they would fall where they should without any manipulation.)

Normally, none of the previous attempts to get them back in the cradle will work. So the final attempt is to turn away from anyone who could possibly be watching (men and tits: they are like magnets for their eyes), stick both hands under the shirt and bra, and then shape them where they should be and snap that bra back down. It works every time. Okay, shaping them only happens when they are big enough to do that. If you have little tits this doesn't apply to you. They have to at least be a handful and a half each. I am not a member of the IBTC (itty bitty titty committee), but some days I wish I were.

Everyone has seen those movies where the guys drool over the women running in slow motion with their tits are flying everywhere. When I see that, I always grab mine, hold them up and moan with agony. I think I have the same reaction as men do when they see another guy get kicked in the berries. When I say berries I mean balls and yes, I call them berries.

Running is another story. I have one question for all those ladies with big tits. How can you run? It hurts way too much for me to. I have to strap those puppies down to where they can't move if I want to go for a run. I mean really strapped down. I have to wear a sports bra two sizes to small to go running. If the tight bra doesn't do the trick there is always duck tape to fix that. Duck tape comes in handy with holding body parts in place (if you know what I mean).

Jumping jacks are another story. Even wearing a tight bra I still have to hold them while doing jumping jacks. I call them Boob-Jacks. When you hold up those boobs, your arms create a shock absorber so when you land they don't hurt. I always dreaded doing jumping jacks in school. My gym teacher always used to say "Put your arms up Anna! Touch your hands together above your head Anna!"

"I can't!"

"Yes you can!"

"No, I really can't!"

"Why can't you?"

"My boobs….They hurt. So much…."

FEARS

I am not afraid of trains or going under bridges. When combining the two, that's a whole different story. I am terrified of going under a bridge with a train on top of it. The train doesn't need to be moving but it is much scarier if it is. There are only two options to solve this problem (I have done both).

1. Stop before the bridge and piss off everyone behind you and wait for the train to pass.

2. Speed up and duck really low while passing under the bridge. (As if ducking will do much.)

Ever since I was little I have been terrified of going over and under bridges. My father always told us to put our hands up in the air just in case it fell on top of us, what sense that made I have no clue, but we always did it. So, now every time I go under a bridge with a train hauling ass over the top of it, I have this uneasy feeling that it might just collapse. Now that I'm the one driving who the hell is going to put their hands up? What a horrible thing to say to a child, I still have nightmares.

Another fear of mine is heights. I hate being high. No, I don't mean drugs. I recently had to fly to California (I didn't pay for the trip, remember I am a broke college student). I convinced myself that planes are really a simulator machine where the window is a TV screen for me to look at. If I'm off the ground more than two feet, I will start to feel higher than a kite and eventually get light headed and have an overwhelming uneasy feeling until I am safely on the ground. I cannot handle being more than a foot off the ground. Maybe that's why I can't wear heels. Wow! I am learning a lot about myself while writing this book. I am learning that I drink way too much wine in one sitting and I can't wear heels because I'm scared of heights. However, I still can't help looking over that those heels that are still sitting in that new box in my closet. Someday I will conquer my fear of heights, maybe after a few more bottles of wine.

Needles is another thing I can't do, well it's not that I can't but I avoid them at all costs. Oh hell no! I can't even look at them without a panic attack starting, in fact thinking about someone coming after me with a needle is causing me to get tight chested, and you know with big tits a tight chest isn't easy to deal with. I'm trusting anyone reading this will never mention needles to me or ask to poke me with one (don't ask either unless you want me to pass out and if you do I hope you will catch me). I have to stop talking about needles for a second. BIG BREATHS.

Don't worry. I'm okay now. There is wine. I will tell you that I tried to donate blood a few weeks back because I find that very important to try and help the community. I failed. I passed out after two minutes. The needle never touched me. The phlebotomist cleaned my arm and that was enough to do it. Crap!

I decided to get a tattoo; I really wanted to get one for a long time (it's a colorful unicorn on my butt and of course he is smiling). The tattoo artist started, I was nervous (only because no one is ever allowed to look at my bare ass) but I was able to "relax" enough (while I started doing the breathing techniques as if I was giving birth, which by the way I haven't so I'm only assuming I did it correctly). I said to him, "That's not so bad for three little needles".

"It's not three needles, it's seven."

"Oh."

At that moment he said it was seven needles all the blood drained from my head, I could feel I was turning white, and I started sweating bullets and then my vision started going grey. I had to take a break before continuing. I was very determined to get my tattoo so the tattoo artist and I started talking about wine and calculus. It went by faster after that.

I try and do something everyday that scares me. Even if it is walking next to a glass railing and looking four stories down to the bottom floor, eating an onion or mushrooms, (yes onions and mushrooms scare me), or capturing a huge spider to put it outside.

I don't do spiders especially if it is one of those big hairy fast ones. The couch is a great refuge to stand on and scream every time it moves and then I scream about how far I am off the ground.

It's important to learn from fears and deal with them head on. It's living life to the fullest isn't it? If we all did something that scares us each day, later on it can be something to laugh at. Like that one time at band camp with the tubas…. It was quite scary (you really had to be there). What's a day like not to laugh or at the very least smile? Life sucks sometimes but that doesn't mean there isn't something to smile about on a daily basis. We should all laugh when we see our bed head hairstyle when we get up in the morning and then pretend we are going to go order a coffee with that style. Maybe that might be scarier than funny, but I bet a while after we can laugh about it. I can see someone not being able to smile because they are constipated but even then it's a little funny. Now if you are a little backed up, I have three prune trees in my back yard. You can have some to get things flowing the right way! But in case you are like one of my friends when every time he puts any type of food in his body, he has to use the toilet within five minutes, then you shouldn't have any of my prunes I really understand you probably aren't smiling a whole lot.

It took me a long time to figure that out how to smile everyday. Now I make myself laugh all the time. I'm sure people think I'm crazy but that is all right with me.

I didn't used to talk out loud to myself but now I tend to do it without realizing it. I think you start talking to yourself the older you get. Apparently I can't hear my thoughts so I have to say them out loud. Last week I was in a store looking at storage units that can fit under my bed.

I was touching a medium sized bin and wiggled it and said out loud,

"That's a little big."

That's a normal reaction to say right? I have heard people talk to themselves while shopping. I took it one step too far. I laughed out loud again and said,

"That's what she said."

The funniest part was there were a few other customers behind me that looked at me that I didn't notice until it was too late. I had my phone in my hand too. I was going to try and pretend I was talking to someone but it was far too late to recover. They were all staring at me and all I could do is laugh, smile and back away slowly. I'm pretty sure they think I have some type of split personality disorder.

Now this paragraph will be a great transition into the next chapter (no peeking!). I wouldn't be surprised if someone stopped reading after I tell you what I'm about to tell you. I have struggled in the past with keeping this hidden for a long time and had the fear of saying this to anyone. I am much happier now that I did and wouldn't change it for anything. Honestly, I wish I would of told people much sooner. You probably know already what I'm about to say don't you?

Yes, I'm a natural brunette. I'm just kidding I'm a lesbian. There I said it! That wasn't so bad! It was much easier to say that than trying to take a crap in a public restroom (see the chapter called The Ladies Room).

Coming out a few years ago was the scariest thing I ever had to do (even scarier than a needle) and the most life-changing (duh?), emotional, heart-breaking moment I have ever had. At the point I decided to come out, I didn't care who knew, who cared or what happened. I was called every name in the book from people I thought would accept me…for me.

The last thing I want to do to someone is offend them. I apologized over and over but that never seemed to help. The only way it would help is if I changed who I was attracted to, and even if I were able to, the same people would still be unsettling. I was told many times how disappointed people were in me. How could I be disappointing to people just because I was gay?

All I can say to the people that don't accept me being gay, it's okay, I understand. How about we have a truths? We both live how we want and don't judge each other? Okay? Okay. I'm glad we had this little chat.

LESBIAN PROBLEMS

After coming out I have met some amazing people. All are very supportive and understanding but they do try to set me up on blind dates (which I try to say no to). There are some issues being attracted to other women. I lack that thing called a "gay-dar". Apparently all straight people I know think I have this ability. (I must have missed that seminar. When is the next one?)

There was this girl I see often in class and

I always thought she was flirting with me. I would catch her looking at me and I "thought" she would smile and start blushing. Over a few months we got to know each other a little better. I could talk about my past relationships so she knew that I'm attracted to women. Not once did she mention she liked women or men. I fell for this girl when I didn't even know who she was attracted to. I was thrown for a loop last year when she said she has never had a relationship and then added there were not a lot of hot guys in this small town. I did have a bit of a crush on her. I hate having crushes because that's what they do, crush you (like a bug).

The most odd experience after I came out was a party. It was a birthday party, a surprise party (for me). Everyone there (all but one) was straight. Now, at birthday parties there are usually presents like, clothing, a watch, bath stuff, you know the normal things you give someone for a gift. I have never had a party with everyone knowing I'm gay. Assuming this was their first time throwing a party for a lesbian, can you guess what the theme was? The theme was gay (really it was gay themed). I don't think it was actually planned but all the gifts sure told me that was the theme. I got a bunch of bright colored things that says, "I'm so gay", "I love rainbows", "honk if you are gayer than me", you know, literally gay stuff. How can someone be gayer than someone else? I didn't know there was a scale. Was I supposed to be asked on the scale one to ten, how gay are you? Don't get me wrong, it was a fabulous party but if anyone sees me on a normal basis, I wear dressier things, not bright jewelry or t-shirts what so ever. These gifts were bright and had rainbows with unicorns. It was the first time getting gay things and I loved every minute opening those gifts (but I probably will never wear this stuff in public. It's far too bright for me.)

Now that I have had that experience and you want to throw me a party, please no rainbows, unicorns, etc. I prefer wine; accessories for wine, grapes to make wine, and an elevated garden bed would be wonderful too (of course its to grow the grapes, but not the normal ones you get from the store, wine grapes). Thanks! You are too kind!

I seem to be attracted the "wrong" woman. Let me explain "wrong". I don't mean some women are better than others, well yes I am but that's not the point. I think there are some women that have better compatibility with me. So, when I say the wrong woman, I mean not compatible for me.

Some women can be difficult, jealous, and controlling. Oh and the drama (I am being told it's not as bad as some guys though). It's hard enough to find a lesbian in my area let alone find someone that had the same interests, habits, and morals as I do. I went on a date to a wonderful restaurant and looked at the waiter while I ordered, I would literally get the third degree. She would say,

"Do you know her?"

"No."

"You gave her a flirty look."

"No, I just ordered food."

"I think you know her. Did you sleep with her?"

"No!"

When the waitress came back the feeling of awkwardness was in all three of us. And that was on a first date. (I'm still single. Call me.)

I did have a friend sign me up for a dating site. She took my picture, created my profile, but damn it I lost that log in information… I still haven't decided if it was on purpose or a joke.

This next problem is a big one in my book and the most funny to me at least. When someone comes out as a lesbian, most straight women think they have a huge crush on them. WHY? This has happened to me so many times. Here is one of my recent conversations with a straight girl.

Me: "Hey, I'm getting a group together to see a movie, want to come with?"

Straight girl: "Do you like me or something? It seems like you flirt with me a lot."

Me: "No…. I'm just getting a group together for a movie…..Do you like me?"

Straight girl: "Oh gross no, I'm straight!"

Me: "That's good, because you are definitely not

my type! So are you coming to the movie?"

Straight girl: "What do you mean I'm not your type?"

I have conversations like this ALL the time. I could get upset over it but I find it comical some straight women automatically assume I'm in love with them. Not the case at all ladies!

I'm going to try to write this next few sentences as "scientifically" as I can. Okay, here we go. My heterosexual friends embark in the assumption that I have knowledge of all other homosexual women on a personal level. The assumption of this previous statement is false.

What I'm trying to say is no, I am not friends with all the people that are gay. The straight people I know think if I know another lesbian we should be together forever. That is so not true. I can only name a dozen, when I say a dozen I really mean a handful, and when I say a handful I really mean two, with myself being one of them.

STEREO TYPES

Everyone stereo types regardless if you think you don't. I do it too. I think we should all come out of the closet, it's okay this is a safe place, we're all going to say it now okay, I'll go first. Hi, my name is Anna and I stereotype, quick now it's your turn, I'll wait while you take your turn…phew I'm glad we got that out in the open.

Most of the time I am just trying to get my gay-dar working. I am a huge chicken when it comes to talking to women. My thought process will go a little something like this.

She looks nice. I wonder if she is gay. She looks like she could be but that's not right to judge a book by it cover. My book cover is awesome. I should tell her about my book and put my number in it. I have to talk to her first before I do that. Dang it. I can't tell if she is gay. I would look like an idiot if I were to ask. Where are my friends when I need them? I could just go make someone else ask. If someone asked me would I get offended? Well no, it's happened before. I could say hi to her and take that information into consideration. I don't want to. Yes I do. No I don't. I should probably say something instead of staring at her. I think I am creeping her out now. I'm so bad at this.

I try not to judge people until I get to know them. And let me tell you, some people put up an act for others to like them. I became friends with someone and she told me she loved wine. We went wine tasting and I asked her what was her favorite kind. She said red. Okay? There are many types of red wine. I knew something was up. I ordered some pinto noir and she took a sip and made this awful face. It looked like she didn't want to swallow it (that's what she said). I knew she didn't like wine. She let me know she only said she liked wine because she wanted me to like her.

Not cool people. Just be your self! I like people for who they are (most people). Everyone wants to fit in somewhere but at the same time everyone wants to be different. I am told a lot that I remind someone of another person. I hope not! I want to be remembered as myself, not another person. I guess I wouldn't mind being remembered as that one chick that loves wine and math a little more than she should.

CELEBRITIES I WOULD LIKE TO HAVE A GLASS OF WINE WITH

I try not to idolize other people but there are a few people I admire. In all honesty, I find it odd when fans start crying over a celebrity. If someone were to walk up to me and start frantically crying and screaming, I would be very scared! Could you imagine that? Yes, I understand it's overwhelming you finally get to meet someone you see on TV in person. I don't think it's that overwhelming to start crying. Keep it together man!

A few years ago I won a back stage pass to meet my favorite band of all time, but I didn't start crying. If anything, I couldn't say much more than a sentence. All I could say is hi and I'm sure I had the biggest smile on my face. Not only because I got to meet them but I actually won something! I never win anything!

Getting to know someone famous sounds a little scary. They are human like everyone else. They have flaws and dislikes just like any other person. I think the scariest thing would be finding out that they are different from who you thought they would be.

I was at a nice vegan restaurant while in California. A guy was there that I didn't know but the manager was sure talking to him a lot. A girl in her twenties asked to take a picture with him. Okay, yes he is in a TV series. I felt bad. I wanted to tell that girl to leave him alone and let him enjoy his dinner. After that happened, some A-list celebrities kept walking in the door. It was someone's birthday. I didn't freak out. I let them be and didn't pay attention to them. That's what you do when you see someone famous! My mother did have a lapse and did panic for a second. She stared for a little longer than she should of but didn't get up to talk to them. (That was much better than what she did a few days before. We went on a studio tour and my mother freaked out like a crazy fan over this famous lady riding her bike. It was so embarrassing. I had to pretend I didn't know my mother. I even tried to find a different seat on the little cart (it was full). I'm not going to say who the celebrity (everyone knows her) was but I know she heard my mother yelling at her. My mother whipped her camera out too and started taking pictures of her. Never again will I ever go on any tour with her.)

Back to the restaurant! The best part was when we left. Okay we actually got kicked out for staying there for three hours. There was only one paparazzi standing outside on the corner. We went up to him and asked who he was waiting for. (I hate these guys.) He told us, I have got to be honest, I have no idea who he mentioned. Apparently it was someone's ex-husband. I said no, there isn't anyone in there. He looked a little disappointed. But little did he know a bunch of people were in there. You are welcome celebrities! I told the paparazzi you weren't in there! I wonder if I could of gotten some money out of him. I should have said, "Give me $300 and I'll tell you exactly who is in there and which door you should stand by". There would have been twenty more standing on that curb if I did that! It wouldn't have been the right thing to do if I did that. So again celebrities, you are so very welcome!

There are a few people I would love to chat with over a nice glass of wine. Instead of naming names and making you uncomfortable and feeling obligated (if you are reading this and are a celebrity), I will open the invitation to you. Do I sound like someone you would enjoy chatting with? Drop me a line, send me a text and let's meet up! If you want to have wine with me, let me know. Have your people call my people and by my people I mean me because I can't afford people like you have (but I do have a friend that I could commission to take my calls for me if I offered her a glass of wine too, yeah maybe she'll do it, I'll get right on that).

One other thing, if you want to have wine at your

place, you must pay for my travel, hotel and food. We can have wine at my house but you might feel a little claustrophobic because my whole house is probably the size of your closet. I will be patiently waiting for your invitation.

JOKE OF THE DAY

I am now a firm believer of the saying "it's always greener on the other side". It is! I looked over my privacy fence into my neighbors yard to see if there are any more strawberries I could steal. And yes, it is much greener on the other side of the fence. His grass was a nice fluffy green that was perfectly groomed. It looked like a green pillow of clouds like the lawns in the magazines. I seriously contemplated hoping that fence and laying down on that fluffy cloud of goodness.

I compared my yard with all of the bare spots and the trails my dogs have dug into the ground. There are even spots where there is only weeds (my whole yard). I have weeds growing as grass! I should start watering my yard a little (a lot) more and plant grass seed. On the other hand, it is a rental.

PRONOUNCIATIONS

Below is a list of words I cannot pronounce at all. People constantly try to help me correctly say these words. I do replace these words with something I can say (that's on the right hand-side). I would be so excited for someone to ask me to say these (not!). How many can you say?

1. Cellular – Cell phone service

2. Single – No, I'm not dating at this time (you can't handle all of this)

3. Signal - Turn the blinker on!

4. Signature – Sign here

5. Social – I'm not much of a people person

6. Jewelry – No I will not buy you earrings, rings, or bracelets

7. Pronunciation – Can you repeat that a different way?

8. Supposedly - Apparently my ass can't fit in these jeans anymore

9. Rural – Outside the city

10. Brewery – Where all the alcohol is made! (Give me that!)

11. Specifically – That thing right there

12. Worcestershire – That whore sauce

13. Entrepreneur – The business owner

14. Association – Organization

15. Regularly - Often

16. Horror – I don't like scary movies

17. Statistics – I'm not going to take that stat class

18. Differentiation- Just get the derivative

19. Sessions – Meetings with other peeps

DOGS

I love my dogs. I can do lots of things around them that I can't around people. The best part of it is they can't tell anyone! That doesn't mean they don't judge me. They do give me that look of *what the hell is she doing?*

One of the things that I NEVER do in front of people is sing. I can't sing, at all. If I sing, my dogs will start crying and try to lick my face (I'm guessing my singing voice is very bad). They are kind of rude when I think about this. If I keep singing they will run to the back door, crying, and scratch at it to be let out.

I do talk to my dogs (is that weird?). Timmy (not her real name) will actually talk back. I have no idea what she is saying, but we are having some type of conversation. My neighbors probably think I'm nuts. I wouldn't be surprised if someone is about to knock on my door then turn around and leave if they heard "Timmy, are you a good girl? Should I do my homework or watch a movie with you?"

"Rooo Rooo Rooo."

"I don't know what that means girl!"

"Rooo Rooo Rooo!"

"Do you want to watch a movie?"

"ROOOO!"

"Or do you want to help me with physics."

"......."

"Movie it is!"

"ROOOOOO ROOOO!"

I do admit I love my dogs very much. I put their needs before mine, which means they usually get my whole dinner. They can be jerks some times with the holes they dig, the drool they slobber and the poop; don't get me started on all the shit I have to pick up behind them, but I love them anyway.

If one of my friends isn't a dog person, guess what, we aren't going to be friends much longer. I think of it this way, if my dogs like you (and they normally love everyone) you better like them too. They will crawl up on your lap as if they were a little kitty looking to be pet. Timmy is the worst. She always wants to be held like a baby. I really like my dogs. They are really great. What would I do without them? Nothing, absolutely nothing! I couldn't imagine my life without them. They are truly wonderful creatures and much better friends than humans (just saying).

ANNA NAAX

SIBLINGS

Younger brothers and sisters are great for test dummies. I tested things out on my sister and she tested things out with our little brother. Back in the day (I feel old when I say that), there was a fun activity called sledding. It was awesome when we were younger but I couldn't imagine how uncomfortable and painful it would be if I went sledding now.

One year, my cousin, sister, and myself

decided that we wanted to go slide down a very steep hill for the first time that winter. There was a little difference from the previous year, which caused us to hesitate. It was a steep hill that leads to a lake and the whole shoreline had properties which added huge boulders to reduce land loss from the rising water levels each year. Before we sled down the hill we went to check out how far of a drop it was from the land to the ice on the lake. It turned out to be about four foot drop.

Both my cousin and me were too chicken to sled down so we turned to our attention to the tester, my sister. We told her she needed to try it out by herself because she if she didn't she couldn't hang out with us (I know, we were mean. I already made that up to her with wine). She gets in the sled and zooms down the hill, faster than we expected. You could hear the snow hissing along the sled and then, it stopped when she flew with the sled off the rocks. They acted like a ramp. She was flying. It took forever for her to land. My cousin and I had enough time to look at each other and say, "shit!" before she landed.

She glided about 250 feet onto the ice. We screamed at her and asked if she was okay. She didn't move very much but she stayed in the sled, which meant we could test her again, just kidding. All we heard was moaning. We ran to her and all she could say was, "My butt!" We all couldn't help but laugh. She was pissed for years after that. Once in a while she still yells at me for it. Oh the memories!

My sister on the other hand tested her "contraptions" on our brother. When our parents weren't home they took out the blender (we weren't even allowed to look at it). My sister would put a bunch of crazy combinations in it like ketchup, pickles, sugar, oatmeal, milk, juice, tuna, peanut butter, etc., and then make our little brother taste it (so gross). She would "try it" herself and say it's so good. Obviously he would try it, spit it out and yell at her. She would then belt out her psycho laugh (it's very scary).

Another time she some how got our little brother to wear her skinny girl jeans. All I heard was screaming. My sister laughing like a crazy old woman and my brother crying out "shut up, let me go change back! You said you bought guy pants for me! These are girl pants! They are your pants!" It was very funny to see my brother in these little girly pants. His calves were so little; I don't know how they could hold the rest of his body up.

PET PEEVES

Many things that drive other people crazy don't bother me very much. I love watching someone get pissed off over the smallest things like people smacking their gum, their boyfriend left the toilet seat up again or even people that talk on the phone in a public bathroom.

Those things don't upset set me because, first off, I give people a strange look if they smack their gum. I will have a look of almost pure horror with my eyes really wide. That usually stops them, if that doesn't work, I will wink at them and gesture, call me. That works every time!

I can have a pretty bad day if I drop something multiple times. Flustered isn't even a great word to describe how I feel if I keep dropping things. In the morning I dropped a bowl, wow. In class I dropped a pencil three times in two minutes, you got to be kidding me. At work I dropped the phone twice on the same phone call, seriously! When I start saying *seriously* from the amount of times I drop things it just becomes funny to me. I might be pissed off that I'm dropping items constantly but at least I find it funny. Again you have to laugh at yourself every day!

Now, for that toilet seat being left up; I'm a lesbian. I don't have to deal with seats being left up! As weird as it may sound, I love to listen to someone else's phone conversation when they are going to the bathroom.

It happened just today! I always try to fill in the other side of the conversation if they don't have it on speakerphone.

"Like oh my god Jessie would you believe what my ex boy toy did last night when we broke up. It was so like re-dick like I don't even like want to tell you."

I'm sitting on the pot thinking *oh please tell Jessie what he did. This is going to be great and probably stupid, but I need to know! I bet his new girlfriend picked him up from your place or he's going to be a baby daddy and she isn't the baby mommy! What did he do? Say it!*

"O-em-gee Jessie, I'm about to lose it and there is like someone else like in the bathroom."

No! Now my cover is blown. I thought I was being quiet enough. I have to get up and leave without knowing what Jessie gets to know!

"Jessie! OH EM GEE Jessie, what am I going to do now? …. Well I don't want to tell you what he did it's too hard for me to say, I can't believe he did that too me. I deserve so much better and he can't have this hotness anymore. He's the one missing out! OKAY Jessie! I'll tell you, jeez girl! I told him I was done with his crap and like told him to leave and he was like okay all calm and shit and like he got his stuff and like left."

Seriously….. That was the news? What a horrible and useless story. I just wasted a few moments of your time reading that didn't I? That's how I felt when I was ease dropping!

I don't have very many pet peeves but the few I do have drive me up the wall and I do retaliate (in a nice way I think). The first is people that are on my tail when I'm driving. I start questioning them out loud as if they can hear me.

"Do you really need to be that close to me? Really? You got about ten seconds before I start slowing down. 10. 9. 8… Wow dude!"

I normally go the speed limit, maybe a little faster. By no means am I going any slower. If someone is riding my tail, think again. I will slow way down. I have gone down to 30 mph in a 55 mph zone, and to make it better, it was a no passing zone (for 7 miles!). You should have seen the look he gave me at the stoplight, it was priceless. I just smiled at him and waved.

Being late is another thing I cannot stand. It's one thing to have something comes up than just being lazy. It's 5:00 pm, you were supposed to be here at 4:00 pm. How can you be an hour late and not call me to let me know? Two more hours roll around, than three. What the hell is going on? I will call you and ask where you are and you respond back with "We are still coming over, Billy wanted to watch this movie."

Really!? Why can't you let me know that time wouldn't work? I don't understand if plans are made at a certain time, why is it socially acceptable to be late for no good reason? Acceptable reasons to be late is a pet getting out of the front door, Bobby put super glue in his hair and now his hands are stuck to his head, or if you are stuck behind someone going 30 mph in a 55 mph with a no passing zone for seven miles because you were tailing!

Three words. Be. On. Time! It's not that hard people. If I have class at noon I will be there at

6:00 am and sit through two math classes, a biology class and an acting class all before my class actually begins. Why do you think I'm so smart? It's because I'm on time!

MOTHER

Am I the only one with a weird relationship with their mother? The answer is no. My sister does too (ha ha). In a "normal" family a phone call might go something like this: hello? Oh hi, how are you? That's good. How are your dogs? What do you have planned this week?

Normal, right? (Maybe for you it is). A conversation with my mother always starts a phone call with her saying, "Yes, this is Thomasine." (I think that's my Grandmas cat's name). She says this EVERY time. There is never a hello when she answers. I don't know where that came from. She just started saying it one day. When my sister came out to visit me our mother would call us all the time. I do recall one conversation but before we get that that I do have to mention something.

I am a terrible liar. If I have to lie, I can't talk or make eye contact. So, with that being said, my sister and I were out drinking (before noon). We had martinis and wine and more martinis and some mojitos. We were feeling pretty good (really good). Then the call comes in. As soon as I answered it I regretted it. But it was too late to hang up and pretend my ass wanted to talk to her when she calls back. By the time I realized I had to go through and talk to Mother, we both were already laughing. We knew EXACTLY what she was going to say.

Mother: "Yes. This is Thomasine."

Me: "Yes…We knew you were going say that!"

Mother: "What are you doing? Are you

drinking!?"

Me: "Yes…. Wait drinking what? We have lemon waaaaaater!" (And there's the lie.)

Mother: "You wine-os! You can't be drinking its not even noon yet!"

Me: "I didn't say we were!"

Mother: "Oh! I know! I know! That's called an all-co! You can't drink!"

Me: "Let me check."

Mother: "Check what?"

Me: "My license, my license to drink. Yup! I just checked, we CAN drink!"

Mother: "That's so bad. What are you drinking?"

Me: "Martinis and wine."

Mother: "Oh. Maybe I'll go have one too, with Father."

Me: "You can't drink Mother…"

Mother: "Well why not? Yes I can. I'm 50! 50! Fifty years old! You two go be wine-o-holics by yourself."

Me: "Waiter! We are going to need another bottle of wine STAT! Okay Mother bye-bye!"

Mother: "What!? Another bot…."

Oops! I hung up (on purpose)!

THE CREDIT CARD

A lot of couples have credit cards. I'm sure one person has checked the monthly bill and accused his or her partner of cheating because of the store that is showing up on the piece of paper. That's not necessarily cheating now if someone has access to the card. (Like their kids.)

My little brother went through a growth spurt in middle school. My mother went on a huge shopping spree without my sister or I (neither of them told us either). When they got home, there were bags and bags of clothing which were all for our brother. It had to be at least $500 worth of stuff. Our brother had the biggest smile on his face. He told us there isn't anything for us in the bags we were frantically digging through.

About a week went by and our brother kept rubbing it in how we didn't get to go shopping. My sister and I had it. Right before the start of school is the best time of year for us- new shoes, jeans and shirts. We usually get a few nice things but not this year. We were planning on getting nice supportive bras that cradled the tits like clouds but no. Our brother inherited "me and my sister's" (our parents) spending money.

We weren't having it. We wanted some new things too. Or at least a nice bra and new shoes! We were in high school where the new stuff mattered, not Jr. High where our Mother's "golden boy" was attending.

We were upset, jealous and not going down without a fight (the ta-tas wanted to be in a cloud!). We decided to take matters into our own hands! At least when Mother was gone and

Father was sleeping.

We planned for days, down to the second how the mission was going to go down. We even practiced each step before the perfect night. First, go on to the websites. Second, get everything we want into the online carts, fill out all the mailing and shipping information. The final step was the hardest. We needed the credit card number.

It was a very risky mission. We had to wait upon the night until Father fell asleep while watching TV. When that night happened we were in full cameo gear and ready to do the impossible (not really, but it felt like it). We knew we could get into deep shit if we were caught.

Father was in the basement and his wallet was in the kitchen. We had approximately five minutes to get the card, get down to my room, type in the number and get that thing back in his wallet before he got up off the couch.

One of us had to keep watch. I think we had some type of mayday call if he got up while the other was grabbing the plastic (it was hoo hoo). I was the one that grabbed the card. My sister was the one watching Father like a hawk from the laundry room patiently waiting for movement and the queue for the mayday call.

I grabbed it, ran down to my room and ordered our new stuff! My boobs were going to feel higher than a kite in no time! We both ended up ordering two bras each and two pairs of shoes.

Everyday after school we rushed home to wait for the boxes before our parents saw them. It worked great! They had absolutely no idea that we got new stuff for school and they paid for it.

Everything was fine until the credit card spending report came in the mail. I know what you are thinking, oh shit. Than again, you might be from Missouri and need some more explaining. All right, when my sister and me came home from school, Mother was in the kitchen looking at a piece of paper and saying to herself *what the hell. I didn't buy anything from there.*

Shortly after, Father came home from work. My siblings and I were all in the kitchen getting a snack and then it all happened. Mother called father over and asked what is this charge from? He looked at it and it was down hill from there.

"You charged $150 to this lingerie store? You have a mistress and you bought her lingerie!"

My sister and I stared at each other like we were deer in headlights. We left what was left of our snack and started slowly sneaking down to my room trying to be unnoticed. It didn't work.

While Mother was giving him the third degree, Father was calmly looking at the bill. Then, without saying anything to Mother, caught my sister and I halfway down the stairs and told us to get our asses up there now. Shit. We got caught. We are so grounded.

"Did you two take my credit card?"

Before we could answer we stared at each other debating if we should come clean.

"Did you?"

I said nothing. My sister cracked and said, "well we needed bras! Our boobs are getting huge!"

Mother was standing behind father. She started laughing with no sound which made me laugh, and that created my sister to laugh. Father looked at us oddly and asked why we were laughing.

"Cause Mother is!" we both said at the same time.

He looked at Mother and we could tell he was trying really hard not to laugh. You know how people try to have a straight face and try not to laugh? They normally have a weird ass smirk-smile-nose flare going on? Yeah. That's exactly what Father was doing.

We knew we were in a lot of trouble. We also thought all the stuff we got online would be taken away too. Father got serious and told us to get our butts to our rooms but he couldn't keep a straight face when he said it. We were totally grounded, but it was totally worth it. My tits thanked me. We got to keep our stuff too. I don't think they ever found out about the shoes we ordered. Shit. I hope they never find out that I wrote this.

THE CAFÉ

I enjoy sitting a cafés every once in a while. I'm at one right now! I ordered a large green tea with a small splash of mint flavor in it. I asked the guy if I could double cup it while I held both my hands out and gestured two little squeezes. He looked at me with an awkward face and his eyes went really wide. I stared back at him thinking he was memorized by my blue eyes like everyone else usually is. The lady and her boyfriend giggled behind me. It takes me a long time to catch on to things.

I told the cashier that it's normally really, really hot and having two cups helps, you know, double cupping. Wow. At that moment (about 2 minutes ago) I realized what I have dug myself into. I busted out in laughter and it wasn't pretty. I have a really evil laugh some times when I get embarrassed. The cashier started laughing and turned bright red.

"No, I don't want to double cup your berries if that's what you are thinking!" I told him while I did my double cup squeeze with my hands.

He turned even redder. The two people behind me were laughing so hard they crossed their legs so they wouldn't pee their pants. I think they were squeezing their legs together too hard cause there was liquid coming from their eyes! It makes my whole day if I can get someone to expel liquid from some type of orifice. I prefer the eyes just because it's easier to clean up.

Now I got my tea, sitting here relaxing. I love to people watch. It's fun to see how people act in public without knowing they are being watched.

There are eight other people in here and everyone seems to either have their faces in a computer or gazing into their phones. No one has any idea I am watching them! This is so great!

There is one guy in the corner with his headphones on and is looking at his phone. Looks like he has some chemistry books too. Doesn't look like his plan to come here and be a productive student is working. Oh gross! He just picked his nose! He's still picking it! He has his finger so far up there I don't know how he is going to get it out. I was wrong he got it out.

Now he is looking at his finger. Oh gross! He totally just ate it! He has to be at least twenty years old. He should not be eating his boogers! Oh no! We made eye contact. He looked at me when I had my disgusted face on. His expression looks scared and now embarrassed. I can't change my facial expression! He totally knows I saw what he just had done. Okay, I need to look away now. We made eye contact for far too long!

The one thing I enjoy about people watching is they have no idea what I am thinking about. I can totally look at everyone and think to myself that those shoes definitely don't go with that outfit then debate if I should go home and change.

I wonder if anyone here has any idea I am writing about watching them right here, right now. What if someone is people watching me people watching other people or even if someone is watching someone else watching me watching someone? What if they also think that my shoes don't match my outfit? I can't tell if anyone is watching me. That guy that picked his nose keeps looking over at me, but he doesn't count. Wait. Another person looked at me. Are they watching me? At least they don't know I am writing about them looking at me. Oh no, two more people looked at me. Maybe I should take my head phones off.

More people are looking! Crap! I had the read to text turned on! I had my headphones on my mp3 player and my computer was saying everything I was typing. I'm getting some crazy looks right now! I am definitely not coming back to this café for a while! Smile, wave and run!

WHAT DO I WANT TO BE WHEN I GROW UP?

Everyone has a dream about what they want to be when they grow up. I don't even know what I want to be, but apparently it's going to be something in engineering.

I wanted to be a veterinarian when I was little. Now, I could never imagine giving an animal a shot or worst case, put them down even if was the "right thing to do". My father would hunt deer and birds than bring them home and clean them. I was so upset that he would kill an animal. I would cry and yell at him. I know, sad isn't it? He would come home and I would peek outside to see if he caught anything and as soon as he unloaded it from his truck I was in shock. He would then explain the deer population is too large and that the deer didn't suffer. No matter what he said I was still upset.

Now that I am considered an "adult", I believe that if you can't hunt an animal yourself, then don't eat it. Just imagine a little chicken, you feed it, care for it, and pet it like a kitty. Can you kill something you get attached to? I can't. I really want chickens! Lately, I have this obsession with chickens. I want to pet one and if they let me, hold one (I will probably cry). They are so cute! If you couldn't guess already, I am a vegetarian and I am slowly becoming a vegan. I love animals. I only want them to be happy and have a great life.

I also wanted to be a singer, but I can't and will not sing. Ever. I sound like a boy going though the puberty stage with the squeaky voice.

I try to sing in my car but end up laughing at myself.

Becoming a comedian sounded like a good idea but I have a fear of talking in front of a bunch of strangers so the next best option is writing this book. If I try to tell a joke to a group I usually mess up and say the punch line before I should, or forget the punch line all together. I am a terrible joke teller. Writing this book gives me time to look at each sentence and make sure it's complete. It also helps me procrastinate on other things like exercising, yard work and even doing my job (my boss doesn't need to know that though). I hope I am succeeding in making you laugh a little with my words of gold.

I wish I could win the lottery too. That would mean I should start buying tickets. There is a very small chance I could still win it without buying a ticket (please baby Jesus!). It's possible but very unlikely. Would you like to see the math behind it? I didn't think so but I might just put that in the back of the book just for you to see but then again maybe I won't.

I dreamt about being a movie star, but I can't

act or memorize lines. My brain doesn't function that way. If I was asked to say one line from this book, I couldn't do it. I will forget I even wrote this sentence right here. Trust me, I even tried to say a line to a friend, it didn't work so I said, "Just read my book!"

I actually went to college for a year to become a live sound engineer. I decided not to pursue a career in recording. Music is my hobby; I didn't want to ruin it by getting stressed about having it for a career. I love music, playing it and listening to it and try to sing it without laughing at myself. I wanted to be a guitar player like my favorite guitarist (he's in my favorite band that I'm not going to tell you about). I'm not a very good guitar player. My fingers are short.

Now, I am studying to become an engineer! I love math and physics. We are learning about some very powerful equations! Love it! I have some great ideas for vehicles that do not run on fuel. How cool would that be?

I love science and learning the math behind it. I am debating about being a mechanical engineer on movie sets. That would be pretty cool to have some experience on that. However, I do think my "calling" is to change the whole automotive industry with new, brand new engines designs. Yes, either help change the world into a more technically advanced civilization or entertain citizens with movies. I do have two other back up plans if those other ones don't work out. One of which that involves me and a reality TV show (and a bunch of single women) and another that involves a daytime talk show. So many decisions, which one should I choose?

ANNA NAAX

WRITING THIS BOOK

It was so hard writing this book. Not actually writing it but keeping it a secret. No one knows except my editors. It's so hard to lie to people! My co-workers can be snoopy and peek over and ask what I am typing on my computer or ask me why I'm swearing quietly and pressing the delete button so many times.

Obviously I can't look them in the eye and lie. I look either at the floor or keep staring at my computer and tell them I'm editing a book for a friend. Now I have to tell everyone that. Crap. I could have said I was writing a boring English paper and slowly shut my laptop screen but no. I just HAD to say the first thing that came to mind. Technically it's not a lie. I do read through my book and edit it. I could find myself to be my own friend. Right? I don't think it works that way.

What's worse is people will ask more questions! Why? It just makes it harder for me to lie about the first lie and than I have to try and remember it all which forces me to lie some more. It's not easy to lie about writing a book. I thought it would be! I want to keep it on the down low. I didn't think anyone would ask so I didn't plan ahead a lie. When I write my romance novel I will definitely have to come up with a cover. Nah. I will just tell them I'm writing a lesbian romance novel and then snap a picture of their reaction and put that on social media.

I hate lying. It's much easier to tell the truth and get the million questions that follow. I don't know how people can lie all the time. How can you not start laughing?

I can tell people who are lying to me by their voice and everyone has a lie face. It's easy to get someone's lie face to show. If you think they are lying, ask them a question you know is true. That's their truth face. Now ask them a question you think they are lying about. Compare that to the truth face. If it's not the exact same tone of voice and facial expressions', that's their lie face! After that just say "tell me the truth, I can tell that's a lie!"

Writing this book has been fun. I highly recommend everyone write one. Let me tell you a little secret. The reason I wrote this book is because of my mother. No, this is not an "awe that's so sweet" kind of moment. I called her up one day and told her I was bored. Her response, go read a book. I don't read, ever and I let her know that too. Her response to that was "well, go write a book". So here I am, finally listening to my mother for one of the first times in history. I know she was being sarcastic when she said it but that's okay.

A little wine did get me motivated to write

my thoughts down instead of randomly laughing at myself about them. I hope you (the reader) have laughed a little, or at least have asked yourself *what the hell am I reading, she is so weird, or this is stupid*. If you haven't, well it's hard to tell you, but something must be wrong with you! I'm just kidding! You are great! I'm glad you are reading this sentence right here right now and you have read this far!

HAPPINESS

What is happiness? Is it having lots of nice things? Or even lots of down time? Can anyone be happy with very little? I will try to explain all of these in this chapter.

I don't know what happiness is fully, but I am a pretty happy person for the most part. I try to have a positive attitude towards everything good or bad. Why would anyone have a negative attitude for something good? I don't know.

Contentment is a good start for me, at least to be happy. I don't have much, but I am content with what I do have. A lot of people despise others with what they have which I can't understand. The only thing(s) that I not so much despise people for having but more drool over is a four door Mini Cooper or a brand new Jeep Grand Cherokee.

When I'm driving in my 90's car (that has more than enough miles to get to the moon) and I see a Mini or a Jeep I say really loud *that lucky sucker!* I don't mean it in a despiteful way, it's just I absolutely love those vehicles and those owners better be taking care of them! That's the closest thing that comes to despising others. I never really want what others have. I don't need those things. A stove would be nice though. My house doesn't have one and I love to cook!

I find it interesting how something that is normal to have is over looked. In every house I have lived in there has always been a stove. Now, every time I visit a friend I always stare at the stove and have flash backs of cooking with one. It's a very emotional moment. Those moments of cooking with my cousin and sister bring liquid to my eyes (not really). I start laughing while gazing at the stove while remembering the good old times. My friends must think I am so weird. I haven't told anyone about my feelings and memories about stoves, so you are so welcome reader, that's one of my deepest and darkest secrets!

I saw this homeless man one day when I was stressing about having no gas and driving thirty miles to a doctor appointment. I was very upset at the world that day because of my situation. I had no health insurance but couldn't miss this appointment for my back. I had no choice but to go and pay out of pocket. This one guy, with one word on his sign really put things into a different prospective for me. The sign said *smile*. He would point at the stopped cars and show his sign to them until they smiled. I quickly tried to dig for change that I didn't have. I had my last $5 in my wallet. When I drove up to him and told him to go get some water and handed him the cash he smiled at me. He said " I don't want your money, I got a smile from you and that's all I could ask for."

I couldn't believe it. This man was so content standing outside in the hot sun making people smile. He was happy.

I felt selfish after that. I had a running vehicle regardless if I could get gas or not. I had clean clothes that I could wash at my home and I was upset at the world? While this homeless man was happy as can be holding up a cardboard sign all day. You can be happy with nothing.

Everyone is such in a rush these days and doesn't see what it truly means to be happy. Are you mad cause you don't have any money to go out with your friends? People get upset so easily. So what if you can't go out. Write a book like me! I can't do very much for the next few months but I'm happy writing this for y'all. Maybe for some of you going to school you should go do your homework and put my book down!

So to answer the questions in the beginning of the chapter, they are: no, you don't need nice things. No, you don't need lots of down time. Look at me, I'm happy and an engineering student. Do you think that happens a lot?

In the end you get one life, would you want to live it pissed off at the world for having very little or be happy for what you got and enjoy it? I can tell you one thing. Wine.

ANNA NAAX

DISLIKES

Everyone has things they cannot stand. It may be some food, people or even words. To start, the words below I dislike with a passion.

1. Moist
2. Smear
3. Vomiting
4. Panties

What a horrible word, moist. Moist. Moist. Panties isn't much better. Moist panties. That's even worse. I can stop now! I'm going to be thinking about that all day now. Gross. It's a good thing I don't wear panties!

He was vomiting all over then I saw a huge smear of it all over my pants that made my panties moist.
Said no one ever!

More dislikes:

1. New shoes
2. Vomiting
3. Moist panties
4. Mosquitos
5. Dog poop
6. Reality TV
7. Computer programing
8. The smell of fresh cut grass
9. Bees (the stinger kind)
10. Running (my tits hurt even thinking about it)
11. Bills
12. Spiders (gross)
13. Dirty dishes
14. Penises
15. Folding laundry

JUST TO CLEAR A FEW THINGS UP

I get asked a lot what I'm going to school for. Mechanical Engineering. The first thing most people like to ask next has something that has gone wrong in their car. Why do people assume I am going to be a mechanic? I do have a response for all of you that are thinking about asking the same thing; no, I cannot fix your car. Take it to a mechanic. I might be able to trouble shoot it but by no means can I fix it. Yes. I do have an understanding how it works. Yes. I do want to get into the industry and design engines, but not fix them. Again, no I cannot, will not, fix your car.

I am not strong at all. I am not by any means saying women are weak. I'm just saying I'm not as strong as some mechanic guys are. I tried to replace my spark plugs once and I couldn't even get the rubber wires off. If you are a woman and can pull the spark plug wires out of my car, I would like to see that. I am not that tall either. I will need a stool or have to park next to a curb just to put oil in my car.

LIKES

I, like many people have things they like and can enjoy. My first like I will tell you about is pretty common. Chocolate. I love Chocolate. The only chocolate I absolutely love is sea salt dark chocolate with almonds. It has to be at least 80% cocoa and the almonds chopped up and mixed into the chocolate. The sea salt gives this salty flavor (I know it's salt) and the chocolate flavor is boosted. If you want to know what I'm talking about, just go buy some. Oh, just so you know it comes only in one of those extra large chocolate bars. It's also going to be a challenge not to eat the whole thing at once.

The best thing in the world is a new pair of socks. Nothing tops new socks. It must be just me but I love putting on brand new socks. It really doesn't matter if they cost a dollar or fifty dollars, well it does. I probably wouldn't wear a fifty-dollar pair of socks but that's beside the point. I love socks.

What do I want for my birthday you may ask? Socks. I go through socks as if they were going out of style. I change out my socks at least three times a day or more. I got to have a nice pair of socks on when I'm eating my dark chocolate sea salt with almond extra large bar!

More likes:

1. Garlic
2. Going commando (no more moist panties with that breeze)
3. Fresh fruit
4. Flat bread
5. Potatoes
6. The color baby blue

7. The color red
8. The color lime green
(Which none of these colors appear in my wardrobe)

9. Physics
10. Playing music (I can play many instruments)
11. Women (Holla!)
12. Lemon Water
13. Wine!
14. Fall (The season, not actually falling)
15. Rollie pollie bugs (they are cute)
16. Cloud like bra's for the ta-tas

ANNA NAAX

TECHNOLOGY

Technology is improving everyday. It's making everyone's lives much easier. Or is it? I can hardly have a normal conversation with someone to begin with. How can anyone expect me to have the attention span with them pulling out their phones to look at it? It's very distracting. I can only do one thing at a time. It's either talk to me or you look at your phone. I can't concentrate when you are doing are trying to do both.

Social skills are going down the toilet with all this distraction in my generation. I don't like it. If anyone reads this and goes out to dinner with me, turn your phone off and have dinner. Okay, I will do one selfie with you than off it goes!

Cells phones are great though. I use mine everyday to check out how many people are following me on twitter. I have two so far! That's two more than I thought I would ever have. Thanks to my two followers! I should re-dedicate my whole book to you (but I won't because I am writing about you right now and I'm lazy).

On campus, I see a bunch of people looking at their phones while walking. One girl ran right into the tree and a guy was hit in the face with a door. How is anyone supposed to see where they are going if they are looking down? If you can't walk and text, than don't drive and text. I make this clear no one can do both by walking straight (and some times run) into them on purpose if they have their phones out. Yes, I walk right into people to see if they are paying attention to their surroundings! Learn from what I'm saying right now, don't use your phone while driving, period! And please stop trying to walk when staring at your phones (you look really dumb and I think social media can wait a few minutes).

TO MY EX'S

I've had better.

FAKING IT

Now, I know for a fact that everyone has faked it in one way or another. EVERYONE. Yes, even you. Yeah you. No don't try to look at the person behind you!

In once sense or another you have fake it. May it be smiling when you are having a conversation with someone you just want to palm smack them right in there face, maybe even multiple times or even with a base ball bat. But you can't. Cause that my friend, that's illegal. Instead we fake a smile nodding our heads as if we are paying attention to what they are saying.

While, in our minds we are saying to our selves, shut your face before I shut it for you. Really you are still talking. Shut it. I wish I could smack you into not talking. I really don't like you but you really don't know that. OMG how much more can I bare! I hope I get struck by lightning.

Have you dealt with someone you just can't stand? Or am I the only one. I try to be nice, civil and treat others the way I want to be treated. But for real! It's hard some times not to say "can you please just be quite, I really don't like you and I rather walk away than suffer another pointless moment of pretending I do." (Note that I get along with 99% of the people I meet.)

We (most normal people) don't want to offend people like that. I hate hurting people's feelings. I feel so bad. Then again some people deserve it!

It's funny though after faking the worst ten minutes of your life (or as it seems), what do we do? Hello social media! That's all I see on there for the most part!

Jessica is - *Having the worst day at work in the history of mankind. I had to pretend I didn't know Betty deleted me. We discussed the weekly budget and what we did this weekend. I wanted to say, "you deleted me wtf!". I can't believe how much of a witch she is. I am so mad right now! I think I'm going to quit!*

We even run to our phones to text EVERYONE in our contact list. Well, maybe not everyone (for me everyone, I only have 7 contacts in my phone). Of course we do run to our closest friends at least the closest friends for that week and complain about the torcher of faking it.

The only time we don't fake it is in the bathroom. Wait I mean the bedroom. I guess you could fake what you fake in the bedroom in the bathroom, if you really wanted to.

Anyway, back it faking it in the bathroom. Damn it! In the bedroom! So, I'm told if you are in a straight relationship, ladies, it's not that hard (that's what she said) to fake it. I think I can explain each step all on the rest of this page! Challenge accepted!

Okay, so when you are in the sack with your man, all naked and ready to go you wait till he touches you……

[Note from the Editor 1: I don't think this section is very appropriate. I will have her write a romance novel for her next book. She did write it all on one page though! Challenge completed!]

See it's that easy to fake it! Now the real skill in faking it in the nest is with another woman. Now, maybe most of you reading this have no interest in lesbian sex (except for some straight men). So let me explain faking it with a lesbian. It's hard, really hard. I mean extremely difficult. It's going to take me at least three pages to explain this!

So if you don't want to hear what lesbians do in bed please skip to the next chapter. Oh! You are still reading! Great! Let the (lesbian) foreplay begin! Alright, so when your girlfriend has…….

[Note from Editor 1: No.]

[Note from Editor 1: Still no.]

[Note from Editor 2: Turn the page…..]

[Note from Editor 1: I need and adult! I need an adult!]

[Note from Editor 2: I think Editor 1 is in shock. I don't think she has ever read a romance novel.]

[Note from Editor 2: Looks like I will be writing the note for this page too. Here we go. Wow! Definitely not PG-13!]

[Note from Editor 1: OMG it keeps going! Turn the page!]

That's it. It's a lot but still, that's all to it. That's a little bit more then three pages. Women are simple but complicated at the same time. I should know, because I'm a woman. I can't believe I just said I was a woman. Hell, I feel so old now! One more thing, I have no experience faking it so you probably shouldn't listen to anything I just gave you advice on.

ANNA NAAX

FRIENDS

Everyone has friends, even me! I know! It's crazy how I, my self have legitimate friends! I have a few close friends and three more closer friends that I tell everything thing to (my dogs, ha). I wish I could paste my text messages in here for you all to read. I know my friends think I am a bit crazy and they say nice things like *I miss hanging out with you sometimes.*

They can be really sweet for a split second

and I will feel special but they always end up ruining it. Their nice compliment will be followed with *other times I wonder how the hell we are friends.* Thanks friends you are too kind. Oh by the way, you suck too! (That's what she said!)

I think a true friend is there for you no matter what and will help in everyway possible. Along with their loyalty and dedication, they are also brutally honest. I mean deadly honest.

"How does my outfit look?"

"You call that an outfit? You look like you came out of a circus mirror!"

"That's a bit rude!"

"You want me to be honest right?"

"Yeah, I guess."

"Go change."

That's not the worst of being completely honest with a friend. It can be a step above to where I had no idea it could be taken.

I enjoy new slang words and/or sayings. I

never really get into the crowd with new sayings but I do find them interesting. For instance, the way I heard of a "selfie" was very, how should I say this, odd. I had no idea what a selfie was until I got a certain phone call. Now the person on the other end asked if I got the "selfie" she sent. The what? She had to explain for about five minutes what a "selfie" was. That's so stupid. What happened to this world? A selfie?

The saddest part was the person who called me was my mother. The same thing happened six months earlier with "twerking".

My computer doesn't recognize the words twerking or selfie. The day it will think they are actual words, I will cry.

Back to the main topic: friends. One situation sticks with me when it comes to friends and honesty. I just had my hair dyed and it was horrible! I invited one of my good friends over to help fix it. As soon as she saw my new hair color she said,

"You look like a ten mile lesbian."

What the hell is a ten mile lesbian!? How

have I never heard of this before? Well, I am an engineering student. That's a horrible joke. She explained that it meant you can tell that I'm a lesbian from ten miles away. How rude right!? But in all honesty she asked me if she was wrong I didn't have a choice but to say no. So she was right.

The part that got me slapping my knee was when she fixed the color. I also had to cut my hair to make it even. Yes, I cut my own hair. I will never get a $4.99 hair cut again! Anyway, she looked at me, tilted her head, and said after a long silence,

"Now you look better, like a three mile lesbian."

"Thank you?"

THINGS MY EDITORS SAY

- Damn it Anna!

- Seriously, I just changed that now you are changing it back?

- I'm going to jump off a curb Anna! A curb! Don't make me do it!

- I don't want to know about your boobs anymore than I already do.

- You remind me of a much crazier version of Ellen DeGeneres.

- Can you at least do a zipper check if you are not going to wear underwear?

- I think you have had plenty of wine.

- What. The. F word.

- You are crazy.

- Yes. Yes Anna, you do make me smile but that doesn't mean you aren't crazy.

- You. Are. Driving. Me. Nuts.

- Can you put some clothes on please or at least a towel, my neighbors don't want to see that!

- You can't spell even if your life depending on it.
  Now if it were math, you just might have a chance (a small one).

Dear Anna,

You are a great friend even if our friendship started because of that crazy psycho ex-girlfriend Samantha. You have been a great friend, even when I haven't been the best. I miss you like crazy! The pride cruise was the best.

Love you lots,

ME [Angela S.]

ANNA NAAX

THINGS I TELL MY EDITORS

- Oh shut your asses, you love me!

- No, I am not wearing underwear right now. Can you tell?

- I need more wine! No don't stop there! Fill it up to the rim!

- Why do I need to spell check? Isn't that what editors are for?

- You. Are. Driving. Me. Nuts.

- I'm changing that back to what I wrote before.

- Is my zipper down? Yep. Hello bush!

- Look at my tits! They are huge right now!

- Can I just make one person in this world laugh? Or at least think I'm crazy?

- How do you like this dance? No, okay.

- Control your tits and everything will be okay!

- I'm not that crazy. Well, maybe a little.

Dear Angela,

You are one of my favorite people of all time. Yes, it does suck a little how we met, but I can gladly say I would do it all over again to have a friend like you. I am deeply saddened that you had to move thousands of miles away. I am glad we are still in touch. I miss you bunches!

Lots of more loves,

A

THINGS MY EDITORS SAY TO EACH OTHER

Hey. How's it going?

I'm good. How's your day going?

I can't complain. Well, I could complain about editing this book. How much time do you have?

Don't get me started!

She wrote a whole chapter about hash tags. WTF!

WINE

I love my wine. My wine loves me (I think). I love it a little more than I should. My sister thinks I have Novinophobia. I can't say that word either. It's the fear of running out of wine. Yes. I think that describes me pretty well. Even if I don't drink it all the time, I must always have an unopened bottle. Trust me, I don't drink as much wine as you are thinking think I do right now. All right, yes, I am drinking wine right now but can you really write a chapter about wine without drinking it?

I did wake up one morning knowing I drank too much wine with my friends. With half eaten wine Jell-O, was the moment I realized I should maybe limit my intake next time (all the time). Yes, wine Jell-O. That was a fun night (I think). But wine Jell-O, not so great at least the next morning. I don't remember eating half of it or even making it! Do you know how long it takes to make Jell-O? A long time, that's how long. And I remember nothing or how this chick ended up in my bed! It kept chirping at me and ruffling its feathers!

It's a little sad that out of most of my friends, I am the only one that likes wine. No one else will drink it, so I end up drinking it alone. When I drink one too many glasses of wine; good luck trying to shut me up. I am fairly a shy, quiet person. That is, if I haven't been drinking wine. For some reason I feel the need to explain something cool in either math or physics. I am aware most people don't think math is cool. I don't know why I think it is appropriate to teach my friends logarithmic differentiation when they haven't even passed basic algebra. Apparently I find it an easy task when I am drinking to explain in detail how different methods in math work so nicely.

When people around me say they don't understand what I am doing, I just go back to the beginning and start all over. Could you imagine a party where the host is drunk off of wine and trying to teach you calculus? If you haven't, you are missing out! Hmmmm. No wonder why no one ever wants to have a get together at my house anymore. That's okay, more wine for me (and more math problems).

My sister and I love wine but sadly we don't live in the same town to enjoy it together. I remember how we opened our parents wine bottles without them knowing about it. We carefully cut the tops off with box cutters with such precision so that if you touched the foil of the wine bottle it would cut you. It was a perfect circle. This is where all my engineering skills started, with wine. Then we screwed in the bottle opener but only about half way (I will explain more about that in a minute). We then pulled the corked off unlike how you are supposed to press the opener against the bottle, we did this so there were no marks left behind and so we wouldn't rip the foil. I don't think Mother knows we did this.

Instead of indulging in our victory and drinking it all, we poured it into another container and tried to figure out how to refill the bottle and make it appear like wine, again without actually being wine. Up until this point, I was golden. My detail to attention paid off and that was all about to go down the drain. We couldn't figure out what the hell to put in that bottle to make it look like red wine. We had pink lemonade mix, cola and chocolate milk. That's it. We went with the lemonade mix first and that was too light so we added some cola. That was a little closer, but still a little off in color. We need to hurry cause Father was coming home soon. What did we do? Poured some chocolate milk in it. Do you know what milk does in cola? It curdles instantly! Its was so nasty looking and my sister said it was good enough they won't even notice!

I plugged the wine bottle with the side of the

cork with the hole in it. Remember? I only let the corkscrew go half way through leaving the other side of the cork flawless like it was never opened. Then my sister carefully dabbed the edges with super glue and I put that perfectly circular shaped foil back on and it was like we never touched it. And that's how we started drinking wine.

FEELING DOWN?

From time to time I do feel a bit down. Those days that you don't want to get out of bed to take on the day seems far too difficult. I am here to help! These steps may help you get through a slump.

1. Force yourself out of bed (it's okay if you cry a little)
2. Take a shower (make sure you undress first)

3. Watch the your favorite funny movie or show
4. Dance as if no one is watching
5. Smile
6. Make yourself laugh (by reading my book)
7. Pet your pet and tell them they are such a cute thing in a baby voice
8. Look at your pets reaction
9. Now take a picture of that face and send it to me! (AnnaNaax@hotmail.com)
10. Repeat step 3

11. Repeat steps 4-6 hourly

Feel better now?

WHAT AM I DOING?

All my friends are out hanging out at bars, bowling, or even having a bonfire (I recently was corrected that it wasn't called a *bomb fire*, it only took 25 years to figure that out). I am usually at home because I can't afford to drive anywhere (my vehicle gets an average of ten miles per gallon, too bad it wasn't $\int_{10}^{13} 2x\, dx$ (if you know what I mean). My peeps call me and tell me to come over while taunting me with wine. Come on friends! You think I am stupid? You don't drink any wine! Plus, I don't have free time!

While they are having a good time, I'm sitting here talking to my dogs asking them *who's a good girl/boy, who wants a cookie, who wants to lay on the couch with me, is that a kitty outside, do you want to go outside, my babies!* (While I was typing all those things, I was also saying them to my dogs. Just thought you wanted a visual.)

It sucks that I'm not hanging out with the crowd but it's also a good thing. It keeps me out of trouble and focused on what I need to get done (like watching reality TV that I hate so much and drinking wine).

So, this chapter is called *what am I doing*. I will tell you what I'm doing. Writing this chapter. You are welcome. I will be here all week. Maybe more than a week because this is my home which I live in. So that means I will be here for an undetermined amount of time which is good for you because I'll be here for more than a week. Sadly I will not be writing this book for that long. Thank goodness! I really want to start on that romance novel and of course get this book out for you to smile and laugh out loud.

THE LADIES ROOM

I'm in the bathroom playing chicken with another lady. My laptop was in my bag so I just pulled it out. I think she really has to take a shit and by shit everyone knows women only poop out roses (I hope there aren't any stems!).

I have been waiting for her to leave for ten minutes! Why do women do this? Better question why do the architects make multiple stalls where you can hear, smell and see everything? Why can't there be a bunch of little bathrooms in the ladies room? I absolutely hate using the restroom in public. I'm sure the lady listening to my type this in the next stall doesn't like shitting in public either.

Damn it, I really have to do this. Damn it squared! Another person came into the bathroom! She is sitting in the other stall next to me. Great now all three of us are playing chicken. Lol the new girl just tooted. I think she heard me giggle. Little do they know, I will win this; I can hold it all day long. I wonder what they are thinking right now.

They are probably thinking how much longer they can hold it or trying to figure out why I am on my lap top typing. I bet they don't know I am writing about them! The new girl left, more than likely to find a different bathroom to let her dozen roses out.

This other chick is tough and she needs to leave, now. I can tell by the sounds she is making she is having a hard time. Oh god is she having sex over there!? No she isn't I looked under the stall and only saw one pair of shoes. I would of shit my pants if she was, well more like in the toilet. I do like her shoes; those are some nice shoes.

I win! She ran out the door! That's right this is my bathroom! Mine! I could of let her expel her flowers in peace; I only came in here to blow my nose.

SHIT GETS REAL

I can totally do a math joke right now. I'm going to do it!

$$(\sqrt{-shit})^2$$

Shit just got real! HAHA!

With all joking aside, life can suck some times. This is what I'm doing in my free time, writing this book. I am a broke college student living paycheck to paycheck. More like not living paycheck to paycheck. The next four paychecks are already gone.

Everyone goes through a tough time that is out of their control. What can you do? Well, what I do is look at the good things in the situation, be grateful for those things, even if you have nothing. I can say, I may not have anything to eat tonight, but I do have a roof over my head, transportation, running water, textbooks, and my dogs are taken care of and are happy. It's the same thing if I can't pay a bill right away, I name those things that I do have and even though it sucks, it's better at the same time. Far too much I hear people complaining about their job and how horrible it is to work there. I really want to ask them, can I have it? Or, can you imagine your life without a job?

Besides, looking at the positive things in a shitty situation (that would be a great rock band name!), another thing to do is ask for help. I know its hard to ask for help, I never liked to. If it's necessary, ask for help no matter what. Yes there might be tears. Yes there will be a shortage of wine for the time being. Man, this chapter is feeling like a downer. Maybe I should spice it up with a joke!

What do you call a vegetarian that has diarrhea?

A salad shooter.

(It's okay for me to say that joke. I'm a vegetarian.)

BLUE EYES

On most days, I have the bluest of blue eyes that people just have to interrupt me and comment on how blue my eyes are. Yes people, I know my eyes are really blue right now. I usually don't look people in the eyes and honestly, I don't talk to people that often. But when I have to, I do make eye contact it's as if they are just staring at my eyes and not paying attention to what I'm saying.

"Ma'am you need a new phone, the whole thing is fried. You can get spare parts but that's going to be expensive for the labor."

"Uh-huh…"

"You will need the serial number and model number to get the parts. Do you know where to find those?"

"Uh-huh…"

"Can you show me where those are?"

"Uh-huh… wait what I need a new phone?!"

"Were you freaking out from my eyes?"

"Yeah…."

I swear if I ever needed a favor from anyone, I could look at them and they would agree to do what ever I asked of them.

"Hey, what are you doing tonight?"

"Nothing, why?

"Want to come over and mow the front and back yard of my house?"

"Yeah...."

"Ok thanks! Come over at six and I'll have it all ready for you!"

"Wait! What?"

People I don't know even stop me. They come to me and make small talk like we have been friends for years, and knowing me, I just play along. Eventually they say I don't know you, but I am just memorized by your eyes. Seriously? Seriously. What do you say to that? All I can say is thank you (but when I say it sounds more like a question. Thank you?). It's so odd to be stopped by a complete stranger.

If you want to know how blue my eyes are, look at the "author" picture in the back of the book. That's my little dog, Lola. She picked that name out to hide her true identity and of course tried to hide she is a girl by wearing that mustache. It didn't work with that flower in her hair.

Anyways, those are my eyes edited on to Lola's face. Are you amazed like everyone else?

ANNA NAAX

A POEM ABOUT NEW SHOES

What can I say about new shoes?
I am drinking wine right now because I choose
The shoes that are wore and torn are what I enjoy
Even though the ones I wear others look and annoy
Yes, I am writing a poem about new shoes
But I can't figure out how to end this line with loose (lol I did it)
This is a poem about how much I dislike the new
And how I enjoy the old shoes even if I say pew
I have to say to new shoes, "I do not like you."

MEMORY LOSS

I almost forgot to write this chapter (not joking). I've noticed I have been forgetting a lot of things. I want to blame it on ageing but I don't think I can (I'm only 25). How is it I can remember complicated equations but yet for get if I shut the back door to the house? I have done that before too! I came home and I walked to the back of the house and the door was wide open.

There now is a need for me to doubt ever

thing I do and don't do. Some of the things I second-guess don't even matter some times. Did I put my car in park? Did I put underwear on? Did I put clean underwear on? Wait. I don't wear underwear. Do I even have a bra on (shit)? Did I put the toilet seat down? Do I have my keys? I need to see my keys in my hand in order to shut my car door. There have been far to many times where I locked my keys in the car and not realize it until it was time to leave.

MATH

Most people hate math with a great passion. You might even be agreeing with that aren't you? I don't understand why. I love math. The only thing I don't like about math is even numbers. I cannot grasp why I don't like even numbers. The closest thing I can say it they aren't ….odd. That was supposed to be a joke. Honestly, I really don't like even numbers. What's even odder than that is my favorite number is 1024.

I am not by any means a 4.0 student, just a nerd that likes math and tries to explain it to the non-math lovers. They never seem to have the enthusiasm I do when talking about math. I get very excited when I explain a problem.

I have put together some work sheets of math for you to do. Have fun!

1.   1+2=

2.   2+2x=4   What is x?

3. $lim_{n \to \infty} x^n =$

4. $\int_{10}^{13} 2x \, dx$

5. $lim_{n \to \infty}(e)^n$

6. Prove that:
    $$(x+a)^n = \sum_{k=0}^{n} \binom{n}{k} x^k a^{n-k}$$

7. Prove that: 2x+1 is always odd for every x great than or equal to 0.

8. Prove the Riemann Hypothesis

9. Explain what hyperbolic functions and show how to get their inverses are and how they relate to the real world.

HASH TAGS

I never could understand the use of hash tags. It took me a long time to understand that the symbol is the pound sign or the ampersand. I strongly believe those automated voices on the phone should say press the hash tag key instead of the pound key. This will happen one day. I just know it. You just sit tight and wait.

I still don't understand what hash tags are used for. My first attempt went a little something like this:

I got over 100% on my physics test! Hash tags for me!!!

Be sides a bunch of laugh out loud responses; the comments I received were very confusing. I was told I am not using the hash tags in the right way. Another person said to type it like this:

#IGotOver100%OnMyTest

I told them no one could read that if I type it without spaces. Why would I put a pound sign in front of a bunch of squished together words? That is not proper English. My whole book is probably far from being proper English but that is beside the point.

Can someone explain this hash tag business? I feel like I am getting old from the lack of technical awareness in social media. My excuse for this: I am too busy doing math. I also could use some training in other social media. I must remind you, my mother had to explain to me what a selfie and twerking are. I still can't believe that - my mother.

MY SECRETS

Everyone has their own secrets. I do have a share of mine that I might be willing to publicize but only if I grab another glass of wine. Okay there we go. It's not considered a glass of wine unless it's filled to the rim. Cheers!

Now what were we talking about? Oh yes, secrets. I don't have very many secrets that you don't already know about but I have some embarrassing secrets. For instance, I go commando a lot, like all the time. I don't know why I still have underwear in my drawer. Well, after this story you will know why I still have underwear.

I finally jumped on the bandwagon and bought my very first pair of yoga pants. They are so comfortable even if I did buy an extra small pair but they were on sale. I didn't know there are sizes in yoga pants, I thought it was one size fits all. Oops. I still love them even if they are squeezing as tight as a boa constrictor. Regardless, I still wear them.

I needed to run to the store but I was much too lazy to change out of my yoga pants. Just one moment, I am going to put them on. Okay! I'm ready! I love my yoga pants. I can see why people wear them in public!

I went to the store with a tank top and my much-loved boa pants when I looked down while in the store and noticed something prickly. Pulling it off my pants seemed like a great idea at the time. Nope, it hurt. It was my hairs sticking out. Wow, this is embarrassing. Unfortunately the yoga pants I have are white and my hair, not so white. I can see why these pants were on sale! Hopefully the security cameras didn't catch me pulling on my own hair. I wonder if the clerk noticed. Now that I'm thinking about it, I think he did.

So, if you wear yoga pants, be sure to either wear underwear for that extra layer of protection or shave it so smooth you could go roller blading on it (or should I say skateboarding?).

Speaking of yoga, I tend to do it twice a day. The first exercise time is between 1:00 am and 2:00 am, and the other about 7:00 am. You must be thinking, *why the hell is she doing yoga at 2 am?*

If you must know I have back issues and I wake up from the pain. I've come to live with it and that usually means doing yoga in my bed. Yes, I wake up and do yoga, in my bed.

If I were to get out of bed and set up the mat to stretch on the floor, I would be wide-awake. I don't want to fully be awake. I want to go back to bed after a quick couple minute stretch. Last night I fell asleep doing downward dog and the night before I fell asleep doing the pigeon. I love that one; it's my favorite.

Now that I'm thinking about doing yoga in the middle of the night; it might explain why I am still single. I do wake up diagonally and hog the bed too. I also let all three dogs sleep on there too. There wouldn't be much room for another person. Hmmm. If I ever have a girlfriend she's going to have to bring a blow up mattress to sleep on.

Another secret, well it's not much of a secret if you were having a conversation with me, I swear… a lot. My friends are kind enough to give me an evil look but I can never pick up on that. I am surprised of the lack of swearing I put in this book. I have a new way to swear out loud and not offend people…as much. I say the first letter of each word.

WTF	BF
WTH	SOB
AH	MF
F	SH

I also say lol, letter by letter. "El O El.". I

could be laughing out loud when I say it too. I hope I'm not the only one that does that!

BATHROOM PRODUCTIVITY

The bathroom. It's the place where my imagination flicks on that non-existent light above my head for another crazy idea. Sitting on that porcelain throne is magic. During those few moments a person can take time to reflect, breath, daydream and push.

I think the most brilliant ideas were made while in the bathroom. I have a notebook in mine just in case, except mine has math, jokes, and more math in it. This chapter you are reading right now was in fact been thought up in the bathroom. I know gross right? I wasn't going to the bathroom; I was putting my make-up on if that helps.

So much can be accomplished while going to the bathroom. I mean sitting down. I don't know how much can get done if you are standing up. But if you are sitting, yes, a bunch of things can get done. Now you do need both hands for some of these things. The laundry could get folded in the bathroom and better yet, most people have air fresheners in there already so just spray the clothing too. You could write a letter by hand or even an e-mail or a book on your computer. You might need to move a desk in there for your computer. Working from home would be awesome if I had a home office in my bathroom! Expect for the phone. I find it weird having a conversation with someone while I'm on the toilet. It's not like anyone really brings their phone to go to the bathroom. Right?

I know a lot of people bring in the paper or a book to read, instead of doing that you can bring my book in there and turn back to the chapter called math and do some homework. With all honesty, the best feeling in the world is going to the bathroom when you really have to go. It's better than chocolate, sex, new socks and in some occasion-better than wine! Think about it, you just had a bunch of water, juice, wine and more water. In about thirty minutes, you are going to have to go but you hold it. Another hour goes by, you start feeling like you really have to go but you can't because you are stuck behind a tractor in Missouri. Now you really have to go. If one more second passes you feel like you are gong to piss your pants. You hold it in by crossing your legs and start breathing like you are about to give birth. Now you are home, you rush inside and run to the bathroom while holding your crotch. Finally, with a sigh of relief. The best feeling ever!

MUSIC

I love music. I have one band I have to listen to everyday at least once. If I don't listen to them, my day isn't complete (or it could be my inability to accept change and not listen to them). I have been listening to this band for many years. I am guessing for about fifteen years now. Oh my, I am getting old!

My music range is very broad. I can listen to just about anything, opera, classical, country, rock to punk, even some pop and dance music. I don't have an actual favorite song, just a favorite band. I'm going to keep you all guessing who it is. I'm going to keep this part a secret just because you know much more about me than you already should!

What would life be like without music? It would be odd to watch a dramatic movie with no music. The kiss sense would just become cheesy without that "romantic" music playing from that violin or the loud dark music blasting when a villain is entering the scene or my dog chasing a squirrel.

That's another career I wanted to do, a score writer. I failed music theory and again I cannot sing, that class was partly graded on singing and finding a pitch. I couldn't do that. Give me my guitar and I could match a note, make me sing it, I will be way off.

IT GETS BETTER

Still alive, still I think:

I have yet to live, for I still believe.

~My tattoo

Up until this chapter I was just trying to get you to laugh. I want to get a little more serious in this one. If I could get the right ambiance it would be dim lights and soft music playing. Lets start visualizing right now. I didn't go into much detail of my experience from coming out because this is supposed (there's one of those words I can't say!) to be a funny book. My coming out wasn't (how should I say this?) all fun and games.

When I first started to hear "it gets better", I could only ask when will it get better? I didn't believe it. Would it ever get better? Everything seemed to get worse. (It does get better).

The days felt way to long and at the end of it I didn't even get one message, call, or email from anyone. I couldn't understand having a phone if there was no use in it. I was very lonely. I didn't talk to anyone or go out to meet new people. The only ones that I could 100% say didn't care what my sexual orientation was my dogs. I knew people were talking about me at work, which did bug me a little but that's what everyone does. Drama and gossip, I like to stay far away as possible.

Eventually I became friends with someone who in the end pulled me out of my depression. I never thought I would need someone. I always thought I could do things on my own, but I was far from right. I met her at my lowest point in my life and surprising she stuck around. If it weren't for her, I probably wouldn't be here writing this book. (This is the point it got better for me.)

I know there a lot of people out there that had a much worse experience coming out than I did. Some of them had their whole lives taken away from them but some how managed to make a better life, a happier one. I am so happy for those of you that pulled through.

It's always a struggle coming out, and I'm not just saying being gay. I'm talking about anyone who comes out with any secret that defines them, a person defining…. thing that someone else can judge. The thought alone of everyone knowing this secret you hold can be over whelming. Repeatedly asking your self, what will they think, will they be mad, will they hurt me, will they stop talking to me, will they try to change me, they might laugh at me.

I've been there. I still ask those things. With people that react negatively to who you are, I believe they don't deserve to be in your life. It's tough thinking about a best friend not being your friend anymore after you tell them this self-defying aspect of your life. If they judge you, were they a good friend in the first place? I don't think so. (But it still gets better. Just because I'm writing this in parentheses doesn't mean you should skip over reading this.)

I've lost a lot of friends over coming out. Some people just can't accept what defines others. I understand that. I let it go and invite in someone who supports me.

Not to long ago, I reached a point where I just didn't care who knew I was gay. I openly talk about it at school, work, and in public. I could care less who knows now. If someone reacts negatively, I can walk away.

People who don't necessarily agree with what defines someone else but still supports them, can still be a good friend (I have lots of straighter than straight friends (if you know what I mean) that support me, I love you all!). The same goes for me, just because I do not live a way someone else does, doesn't mean I should judge them. I think the pressure of society is too focused on judging and labeling people. I think people are people and that's what they should be labeled as....human.

What I'm trying to say is, it gets better! It might not feel like it now but it will. Hold on, it can get bumpy at times but keep holding on because it will get better.

THANK YOU

I found that each person gives you something different.
Each person gives you something to take along the road of life.
None of that should ever be taken for granted.

~ A. W.

You've made it to the last chapter! I can't believe this is the end! I have never been able to read a whole book unless I was forced to! Now look at me, I'm almost done with writing my first book!

I would like to take a moment (this whole chapter) to thank some special people that gave me the courage and inspiration to write this book. I will keep it short and thank a few people.

First off, I would like to thank you. Yes, you the reader! I'm glad you decided to read my book instead of that sex novel you were eye-balling, wait, that's not what they are called. Oh yes, a "romance" novel. I am not looking to be on the best-seller list or even a good review, again I wrote this to make you laugh! I hope I succeeded. If I did, I would love to see you laughing! Send me a picture at AnnaNaax@hotmail.com and who knows, I might write you back!

One of my dear friends said that quote in the beginning of this chapter. I believe that is completely true. It is now one of my favorite quotes of all time. No matter how someone impacted your life, it may be in a good way or a bad one. Each person gives you something to learn from. We sometimes take these experiences in a hard way, but in the end, we get something from each situation and learn from it. Thank you Amanda for being such a great friend!

Now this next woman I'm about to thank is one of the few reasons I decided to publish this book. I don't know her personally nor have I have even met her. All I know is that she is an inspiration to many people around the world and she definitely makes this world a better place (sorry Oprah, I'm not talking about you, but you are a marvelous lady too!). I wrote a thank you letter to her in here (because I don't know her address because that would be called a stalker).

Dear Ellen DeGeneres,

I would like to take a moment and personally thank you. Thank you. If I ever get the privilege to meet you I will bow down to my knees at your royal-es-ness (seriously, I'm not joking!). This world needs more people like you. I might be jumping to conclusions, but I think everyone could agree with that pervious sentence. Again, thank you for the inspiration and happiness you bring to this world.

P.S. I finally started reading your latest book. I'm halfway done! It's only taken me three months!

P.P.S. This will be the first book I read of yours (don't be mad!)

P.S. x3. I haven't read a book in years!

P.S. x4. I love your show! I wish I could watch it more!

P.S. x5. Call me! Lets go grab a glass of wine!

Sincerely,

Anna

The next people I would like to thank are my editors. If my gals didn't help me with this book it would of ended up like this:

And then that one time last year when this one thing happened I was like whoa, and everyone else was like wtf and lol-ing and it was so funny but you had to be there when I got on that stripper pole (and yes, I sure got on that pole!).

Thank you gals for making this

book possible. I hope you enjoyed editing this book as much as I loved writing it! We need to see each other soon! I'll be bringing the wine! Little sister, you are invited too! Lets get our wine on!

This is it! This is the last paragraph! Now that you are almost done remember a few things about me: I like wine, if you throw a surprise party I would like more wine and socks, I like not wearing under wear, and I laugh everyday. I'm trying to figure out what to do after I'm done with this. I do have three loads of laundry to fold. That's not going to be fun. Thank you all so much for everything you have given me! That means you too; yes you, the one reading this. You bought this book, which helps me pay my bills. This has been a great journey writing this book. Take care everyone! Bye bye!

ABOUT THE AUTHOR

ANNA NAAX is a student studying some crazy math equations along with physics. She is born and raised in the United States, which she resides. She has no kids, besides her dogs, and is single. All the single ladies should give her a call.

Made in the USA
Charleston, SC
21 June 2016